KORE
COOKBOOK

Authentic Food from Korea
in 75 Easy Recipes

Maya Zein

© **Copyright 2021 by (Maya Zein) - All rights reserved.**

This document is geared towards providing exact and reliable information in regards to the topic and issue covered. The publication is sold with the idea that the publisher is not required to render accounting, officially permitted, or otherwise, qualified services. If advice is necessary, legal or professional, a practiced individual in the profession should be ordered.

- From a Declaration of Principles which was accepted and approved equally by a Committee of the American Bar Association and a Committee of Publishers and Associations.

It is not legal in any way to reproduce, duplicate, or transmit any part of this document in either electronic means or in printed format. Recording of this publication is strictly prohibited and any storage of this document is not allowed unless with written permission from the publisher. All rights reserved.

The information provided herein is stated to be truthful and consistent, in that any liability, in terms of inattention or otherwise, by any usage or abuse of any policies, processes, or directions contained within is the solitary and utter responsibility of the recipient reader. Under no circumstances will any legal responsibility or blame be held against the publisher for any reparation, damages, or monetary loss due to the information herein, either directly or indirectly.

Respective authors own all copyrights not held by the publisher.

The information herein is offered for informational purposes solely, and is universal as so. The presentation of the information is without contract or any type of guarantee assurance.

The trademarks that are used are without any consent, and the publication of the trademark is without permission or backing by the trademark owner. All trademarks and brands within this book are for clarifying purposes only and are the owned by the owners themselves, not affiliated with this document.

Contents

INTRODUCTION 8

CHAPTER 1: KOREAN BREAKFAST RECIPES 11

1.1 Korean Rice Cakes 11

1.2 Korean Strawberry Milk 13

1.3 Korean BBQ Sauce 14

1.4 Korean Dalgona Coffee 15

1.5 Kimchi Pancakes 16

1.6 Korean Stir-Fried Noodles 17

1.7 Korean Braised Potatoes 19

1.8 Citron Tea 20

1.9 Korean Sweet Potato Latte 21

1.10 Korean Toast 22

1.11 Banana Milk 23

1.12 Korean Pumpkin Porridge 24

1.13 Barley Tea 25

1.14 Korean Seafood and Green Onion Pancakes 26

1.15 Kelp Noodle Salad 28

CHAPTER 2: KOREAN LUNCH RECIPES 29

2.1 Korean Fried Chicken 29

2.2 Korean Chicken and Crispy Rice 31

2.3 Spicy Korean Tofu 32

2.4 Korean Beef Short Ribs 34

2.5 Beef Bulgogi 36

2.6 Korean Beef Tacos 37

2.7 Gochujang Grilled Cheese 39

2.8 Kimchi 41

2.9 Spicy Radish Salad 42

2.10 Korean Fried Rice 43

2.11 Kimchi Soup with Canned Tuna 44

2.12 Yukgaejang (Spicy Beef Soup) 46

2.13 Korean Spicy Squid Rice Bowl (Ojingeo Deopbap) 47

2.14 Grilled Gochujang Chicken Recipe 50

2.15 Japchae (Korean Glass Noodle Stir Fry) 52

CHAPTER 3: KOREAN DINNER RECIPES 54

3.1 Noodles with Chilled Tomato Broth 54

3.2 Kimchi Udon with Scallions 56

3.3 Grilled Chili-Lemongrass Short Ribs with Pickled Daikon. 57

3.4 Tteokguk (Good Luck Cake Soup) 58

3.5 Gochujang with Scallion Grilled Chicken Wings 59

3.6 Instant-Pot Kimchi Coleslaw and Korean Chili-Braised Brisket 60

3.7 Gochujang-Braised Chicken and Crispy Rice 62

3.8 Spicy Korean Steak Tacos with Kimchi 63

3.9 Korean-Style Grain Bowls with Spicy Marinated Steak.....64

3.10 Spicy Kimchi Tofu Stew..66

3.11 Beef Short Ribs Satay (Satay Kra-Toog Ngua) 68

3.12 Spring Bibimbap 70

3.13 Butter Mandu (Butter Dumplings) 72

3.14 Bo Ssäm Grilled Pork and Pickled Slaw in Lettuce Cups .73

3.15 Mochi-Covered Strawberries...74

CHAPTER 4: KOREAN SNACKS AND DESSERT RECIPES 76

4.1 Korean Coleslaw 76

4.2 Korean Egg Bread 78

4.3 Korean Popcorn Chicken 80

4.4 Korean Mochi Doughnut Holes..82

4.5 Sweet Pancake...84

4.6 Korean Fish Cake Soup..85

4.7 Tteokbokki 86

4.8 Easy Baked Yagkwa 87

4.9 Hotteok (Korean Sweet Pancakes)....................................89

4.10 Paleo Songpyeon Recipe 91

CHAPTER 5: VEGETARIAN KOREAN RECIPES 93

5.1 Minari..93

5.2 Broccoli with Tofu 94

5.3 Crunchy Nut Candy 96

5.4 Stir-Fried Oyster Mushrooms 97

5.5 Seasoned Seaweed 98

5.6 Sweet and Crunchy Tofu 99

5.7 Healthy Vegetable Rice Bowl 100

5.8 Stir-Fried Noodles and Vegetables 102

5.9 Vegetarian Kimchi 104

5.10 Korean-Style Mapo Tofu 106

5.11 Crispy Seaweed Noodle Rolls 108

5.12 Extra-Strong Fermented Soybean Paste 110

5.13 Knife-Cut Noodle Soup with Red Beans 111

5.14 Steamed Perilla Leaves 113

5.15 Omija Punch with Pear 114

5.16 Beet Jelly Candy 115

5.17 Vegetable and Fruit Water Kimchi 116

5.18 Spicy Stuffed Steamed Eggplant 117

5.19 Spicy, Chewy, Sweet & Sour Cold Noodles 118

5.20 Braised Lotus Roots 119

CONCLUSION 121

Introduction

Korean food's products consist of vegetables and grains, but fish and shrimp have been used in seas areas. Herbal medicines such as ginger, spring onions, and red pepper have also been used to improve taste and contribute to the beneficial effects of food. In maintaining the food as mentioned above resources, including vegetables, legumes, and fish, Korean fermented technology has played an essential role. Grains, namely rice, and beans have historically been the principal source of starch. Legumes and seafood gave protein. A primary supply of fat was vegetable oils made of soybean or perilla.

Korean cuisine has a history that goes decades back. Since 300 BC, Chinese culture has been strongly influenced, notably by practical treatment. Health is the state of equilibrium, according to Taoist theory, in which food options are essential, and the body of an individual is only safe when Yin-Yang and the five elements are in balance. Yin and Yang are the spiritual qualities that create harmonious shades (red, green, white, yellow, and black) of the five components (metal, wood, earth, fire, and water) which form everything in the universe, include our wellbeing. Therefore, a typical Korean table contains dishes or garnishes made up of five colors, mostly low in calories and abundant in veggies. Today, the principle that encourages the intake of five vegetable and fruit parts and is also widely recommended globally is a philosophy and practice known in Korea since prehistoric times.

A Korean meal is not sequentially presented in a moment layout of appetizer, salad or soup, and main course. Instead, in a "space-based" system, all meals are arranged on a table simultaneously.

Therefore, Korean food is not a simple table arrangement in which individual eats only that is put next to them, but the sharing table that every member celebrates with one another. The Korean food does not include simple meals available but is an "involved" table where each person can choose whatever anyone wants from the various foods on the menu. These Korean meal features contributed to a particular culinary tradition.

There are also plenty of vegetables in each meal, and most materials possess in the form of kimchi-robustly seasoned vegetables fermented. In addition to supplying phytonutrients and protein, lactobacillus and other "good bacteria are also produced by Kimchi that some specialists claim may help improve defense mechanisms. Kimchi is also lavishly flavored with garlic and green onions and plenty of chili pepper, which provides capsaicin, a nutrient shown to safeguard blood vessels and improve metabolism, typically made from lettuce and radish-vegetables in the leukemia cruciferous community. That said, much of a positive thing can be detrimental: heavy intake of Kimchi, probably due to the salts and nitrates it includes, has been linked with an increased incidence of stomach cancer.

Traditionally, Korean meals were prepared with bap (boiled rice), Kuk (bouillon dishes), Kimchi, and banchan (side meals) to be eaten at the very same time. Koreans preferred to use fermentation, blanching, boiling, seasoning, and pickling because conventional baking or frying was not typical cooking practice. The most characteristic process of these techniques is fermentation. The fermentation process enhances the flavor and texture and protects foods.

Korean food also provides several other medical benefits, putting aside the fact that Korean food contributes itself well to a non-obese community. Once the products, seasonings, and methods used, and the cooking instruments, techniques, and innovations applied are considered, such advantages to good health would not sound surprising. This book, "Korean Cookbook," consists of five chapters with a detailed introduction to Korean recipes. Read this book and give your meals a Korean touch with its unique flavors and cooking methods.

Chapter 1: Korean Breakfast Recipes

1.1 Korean Rice Cakes

Cooking Time: 30 minutes
Serving Size: 3

Ingredients:
- 1 tablespoon corn syrup
- 1 tablespoon minced garlic
- 1 tablespoon soy sauce
- 2 tablespoons sugar
- 3 teaspoons chili pepper flakes
- 1-pound tteokbokki
- 3 tablespoons chili pepper paste
- 2 scallions
- 3 cups anchovy broth
- 1 sheet eomuk

Method:
1. Make a broth with anchovies.
2. In a big pan, pour the anchovy broth.
3. Combine the sauce ingredients in a mixing bowl.
4. Over medium-high heat, bring it to a boil.
5. Place the rice cakes on top.
6. Cook, occasionally stirring, until the rice cakes are extremely soft and the sauce has thickened.
7. Combine the veggies and fish cakes in a large mixing bowl.

8. Continue to cook for another 4 to 6 minutes, stirring frequently.//
9. As needed, add additional broth or water.
10. Taste the sauce and, if necessary, adjust the seasoning. Serve right away.

1.2 Korean Strawberry Milk

Cooking Time: 10 minutes

Serving Size: 2

Ingredients:

- ¾ cup fresh strawberries
- 2 cups any milk
- ¼ cup sugar
- 1 ¼ cups strawberries

Method:

1. Using a mixer, stick blender, or masher, blend the 1¼ cups of strawberries.
2. Combine the strawberry pulp, honey, and a third of the chopped strawberry pieces in a small saucepan.
3. Pour half of the chilled strawberry mixture and half of the leftover chopped strawberry chunks into two 16-ounce glasses.
4. After that, pour half of your favorite milk into each cup and serve right away.

1.3 Korean BBQ Sauce

Cooking Time: 10 minutes
Serving Size: 4

Ingredients:

- 1 tablespoon cornstarch
- 1 tablespoon water
- 1 teaspoon Asian sesame oil
- 1 ½ teaspoon black pepper
- 1 tablespoon chili-garlic sauce
- 1 teaspoon fresh ginger
- 1 cup soy sauce
- 2 tablespoons garlic
- 1 tablespoon rice wine vinegar
- ¾ cup dark brown sugar

Method:

1. In a saucepan, combine the sesame oil, black pepper, garlic, red wine vinegar, hot sauce, ginger, soy sauce, and garlic powder; bring to a simmer.
2. In a small dish, whisk mixed cornstarch and water until its cornstarch combines; add a simmering soy sauce combination.
3. Reduce stirring occasionally and simmer for 3 to 5 minutes, or until the sauce has thickened.

1.4 Korean Dalgona Coffee

Cooking Time: 5 minutes

Serving Size: 1

Ingredients:

- ¾ cups milk
- ice cubes (optional)
- 1 tablespoon sugar
- 1 tablespoon hot water
- 1 tablespoon instant coffee

Method:

1. In a mixing dish, mix instant coffee, sugar, and boiling water.
2. Combine them thoroughly.
3. Whisk it on high speed with a handheld mixer until the espresso mixture forms a firm peak (2-4 minutes).
4. In a cup, place the ice cubes and then pour in the milk.
5. Place the whipped coffee over the milk using a spoon. Serve.

1.5 Kimchi Pancakes

Cooking Time: 50 minutes
Serving Size: 8

Ingredients:

- 4 tablespoon grapeseed
- 3 tablespoon unseasoned rice
- 1½ cups kimchi
- 4 scallions
- ¼ cup soy sauce
- ¾ cup all-purpose flour
- 1 tablespoon kimchi brine
- 1 large egg

Method:

1. In a medium mixing dish, crack 1 egg.
2. Whisk together 1 tablespoon kimchi brine, 1 tablespoon soy sauce, and ¼ cup water.
3. ¾ cup + 1 tablespoon flour, whisked in 1 tablespoon melted butter.
4. In a large nonstick skillet, heat the oil over medium-high heat. ¼-cupfuls of batter should be placed on opposing sides of the skillet.
5. Fry pancakes until lightly browned on the first side, about 2–3 minutes, then turn and cook for another 2–3 minutes.
6. Allow cooling completely on a wire rack.

1.6 Korean Stir-Fried Noodles

Cooking Time: 45 minutes

Serving Size: 4

Ingredients:

- Black pepper
- Toasted white sesame seeds
- Sesame oil
- Kosher/sea salt
- 12 oz fresh spinach
- 14 oz Korean sweet potato noodles
- ½ lb. beef
- ¼ bell pepper
- 2 large eggs
- 5 shiitake mushrooms
- ½ carrot
- ½ onion

Seasonings for Beef

- ½ tablespoon mirin
- 1 clove garlic
- 1 tablespoon sugar
- ½ tablespoon sesame oil
- 1 tablespoon Korean soy sauce

Method:

1. Gather all of the necessary materials.
2. Combine the beef spices in a medium mixing dish and stir everything together.

3. Toss in the meat to evenly coat it. Set aside for at least ten minutes to marinate.
4. In a large skillet, heat 1 tablespoon sesame oil over medium heat.
5. Pour the beaten eggs into the pan and stir them around.
6. Sauté the onion with a sprinkle of salt until soft.
7. Repeat the procedure with the shiitake mushrooms, onion, and green onions in the same frying pan.
8. Once the omelet is cold enough to handle, wrap it up and cut it into thin ribbons before setting it aside.
9. Bring a big saucepan of water to a boil with 1 teaspoon of salt in it.
10. Cook for approximately 10-15 seconds after adding the spinach.
11. Whisk together all of the sauce ingredients in a small bowl.
12. The noodles, pour the sauce.
13. To allow the noodles to absorb the sauce, combine the sauce and noodles first.
14. Then combine the stir-fried veggies and meat with the noodles.

1.7 Korean Braised Potatoes

Cooking Time: 30 minutes
Serving Size: 4

Ingredients:
- ¼ medium onion
- 1 tablespoon cooking oil
- 1 carrot
- 3 green chili peppers
- 1.5 pounds potatoes

Braising Liquid
- 1 teaspoon sesame oil
- ½ teaspoon sesame seeds
- Pinch black pepper
- ¾ cup water
- 1 tablespoon corn syrup
- 1 teaspoon garlic
- 1 tablespoon sugar
- 1 tablespoon rice wine
- 3 tablespoons soy sauce

Method:
1. Combine all of the braising cooking liquid in a small dish, except the soy sauce and seeds.
2. Stir everything together well.
3. Cook the potato in sunflower oil in a nonstick skillet (or a small saucepan) over medium-high heat for 5 - 6 minutes.

4. Bring the sauce mixture to a boil over high temperature.
5. Place the carrot slices in the pot.
6. Boil for another 3 minutes after adding the green beans and onion.
7. Even after they've been cooked, the potatoes will remain to soak up the sauce.
8. Add the soy sauce and sesame seeds and mix well.

1.8 Citron Tea

Cooking Time: 20 minutes

Serving Size: 15

Ingredients:

- 240g white sugar
- 240g yuzu fruit

Yuja Tea

- 1 cup water
- 2-3 teaspoon Yuja-Cheong

Method:

1. In a saucepan of hot water, sterilize a plastic container.
2. In a mixer or blender, combine the Yuja pulp and liquid (and not the rind).
3. In a clean dish, combine the chopped Yuja and sugar and stir thoroughly.
4. Close the jar and let it aside at room temperature to dissolve the sugar.
5. Place the jar in the refrigerator until it is finished.

6. The flavor of the marmalade increases with time.

1.9 Korean Sweet Potato Latte

Cooking Time: 53 minutes

Serving Size: 3

Ingredients:
- Cinnamon powder
- Crushed nuts
- 1 tablespoon raw sugar
- Frothed warm milk
- 2 cups milk
- 200g roasted sweet potato

Method:
1. In a blender, mix the roasted butternut squash and milk.
2. Blend until completely smooth.
3. Fill a small saucepan halfway with water and add the sugar.
4. Cook over medium-low heat, constantly whisking, until the mixture heats up (approximately 5 minutes).
5. Distribute the servings among the cups.
6. Add frothed milk, cinnamon powder, and nuts of your choice to finish (optional).
7. Serve right away.

1.10 Korean Toast

Cooking Time: 25 minutes
Serving Size: 1

Ingredients:

- 1 tablespoon ketchup
- 1 tablespoon mayonnaise
- ⅓ cup julienned carrot
- 2 smoked hams
- 1 Cheddar cheese
- 2 thick white bread
- ½ teaspoon white sugar
- 1 cup green cabbage
- 2 large eggs
- 3 tablespoons salted butter
- 1 pinch cayenne pepper
- ½ teaspoon kosher salt
- ¼ teaspoon black pepper
- 1 stalk green onion

Method:

1. Combine the carrots, cabbage, spring onions, garlic powder, cayenne pepper, and salt in a large mixing bowl.
2. Set aside after thoroughly mixing the eggs with a fork.
3. In a nonstick skillet, melt 2 tablespoons of oil over moderate flame.

4. In the same skillet, melt the leftover butter over medium-high heat.
5. Toss in the cabbage combination.
6. Cook for approximately 3 minutes on the other side after splitting the rectangle in half and cooking until lightly browned.
7. Sauté the ham in the same medium bowl until it begins to sizzle.
8. Turn the ham over and top with sharp cheddar.
9. Cook for 1 minute or until the cheese has melted.
10. Squeeze mayonnaise and ketchup over the ham on the sandwich.
11. Serve with the remaining piece of bread on top, sliced in half.

1.11 Banana Milk

Cooking Time: 10 minutes

Serving Size: 1

Ingredients:
- 1 tablespoon maple syrup
- 1 drop vanilla extract
- ½ cup milk
- ½ cup water
- 1 banana

Method:
1. In a blender, mix all of the items and mix until smooth and milky.
2. Serve right away.

1.12 Korean Pumpkin Porridge

Cooking Time: 35 minutes

Serving Size: 6

Ingredients:
- 3 tablespoons sugar
- ½ teaspoon fine sea salt
- ¼ cup sweet rice flour
- 3 tablespoon water
- 3 cups water
- 1.7kg butternut squash

Rice Cake Balls
- ¼ teaspoon fine sea salt
- 4 tablespoon hot water
- ½ cup sweet rice flour

Method:
1. Steam the pumpkins in a steamer over rising hot water until they are tender and soft.
2. In a blender, combine the pumpkins, 3 cups liquid, honey, and salt.
3. Puree it in a blender until it's completely smooth.
4. In a small mixing dish, combine the sweet corn starch and the liquid (3 tablespoons).
5. Warm or cold oatmeal may be offered.
6. Mix the sweet rice sifted flour in a mixing bowl.
7. Make a large dough, then roll it out into a long, thin cylinder.
8. In a small saucepan, bring some water to a boil.

9. Using a sieve, remove the sweet potato balls and place them in a basin with (cold) water. Set away until required.

10. Serve with pumpkin porridge as a garnish.

1.13 Barley Tea

Cooking Time: 15 minutes

Serving Size: 10

Ingredients:

- 3 tablespoon barley grains
- 2 liters water

Method:

1. In a kettle (pot), bring the water to a quick boil.
2. In a pan or saucepan, bring the water to a fast boil.
3. Boil for another 5 minutes on low- medium heat with the roasted barley (in even a tea sieve vessel if you have one).
4. Cool the tea before pouring this into a jug.
5. Refrigerate until ready to use.

1.14 Korean Seafood and Green Onion Pancakes

Cooking Time: 30 minutes

Serving Size: 2

Ingredients:

- 1 red chili
- 6 tablespoon cooking oil
- A few sprinkles of black peppers
- 1 egg, beaten
- 100g calamari
- 100g prawns
- 1 cup plain flour
- 1 cup water
- 12 green onions
- 1 tablespoon cornstarch
- 1 1/8 teaspoon garlic powder
- 1 1/8 teaspoon onion powder
- 1 1/8 teaspoon fine salt

Method:

1. Add flour, cornmeal, white pepper, garlic salt, smoked paprika, and ice-cold water to a medium mixing bowl.
2. Preheat the deep fryer over high heat and drizzle in the cooking oil.
3. Into the pan, pour a little amount of pancake batter.

4. Place 6 green onion tops parallel to one another on the pancake batter and pour a little amount of the batter over and between the bell peppers, covering the spaces.
5. Turn the heat down to medium.
6. On top of the green onions, scatter some squid, shrimp, and red chilies (recommended).
7. Using a knife, cut the pancake into bite-size pieces.
8. Serve with a dipping sauce made from Korean pancakes.

1.15 Kelp Noodle Salad

Cooking Time: 25 minutes

Serving Size: 6

Ingredients:

- 1 tablespoon raw sugar
- ¼ teaspoon fine sea salt
- 60g crab sticks
- 1 tablespoon white vinegar
- 300g kelp noodles
- 60g carrots
- 80g cucumber

Dressing

- 1 tablespoon raw sugar
- 5 tablespoons mayonnaise

Method:

1. Kelp noodles should be washed under cold water and drained for ten minutes.
2. In a mixing dish, combine the kelp noodles, white vinegar, sugar syrup, fine white pepper, and marinate for ten minutes.
3. When ready, combine the cucumbers, onions, crabs claws, and salad dressing in a mixing dish and thoroughly combine.

Chapter 2: Korean Lunch Recipes

2.1 Korean Fried Chicken

Cooking Time: 1 hour
Serving Size: 4

Ingredients:
For Sauce

- ¼ cup honey
- 2 tablespoon packed brown sugar
- 1 tablespoon rice vinegar
- 1 tablespoon low-sodium soy sauce
- 3 tablespoons butter
- ¼ cup gochujang
- 2 tablespoons ketchup
- 1 tablespoon ginger
- 3 cloves garlic
- 5 small dried red chilis

For Wings

- 1 tablespoon ginger
- ½ cup cornstarch
- ½ teaspoon garlic powder
- 2 lb. chicken wings
- Vegetable oil
- ½ teaspoon black pepper
- ½ teaspoon baking powder

- 1 teaspoon kosher salt

For Garnish

- 1 tablespoon sesame seeds
- 1 green onion
- ½ cup cocktail peanuts

Method:

1. Heat four to eight cups hemp seed oil to 275° in a deep saucepan over medium-high heat.
2. Mix salt, cayenne, baking powder, and fresh basil in a small basin.
3. Rub with fresh ginger and a salt-and-pepper combination.
4. Toss legs with cornstarch in a large mixing basin and crush to compact coating onto each wing.
5. Carefully place wings in the oil and fry until the skin is lightly crisped and brown, approximately 15 to 18 minutes, turning with tongs as needed.
6. Butter, powdered chilis, onion, and garlic in a small saucepan until aromatic, about 2 minutes.
7. Cook until soy sauce, ketchup, wine, and miso have bubbled up.
8. Cook, constantly stirring, until the honey and cinnamon have dissolved and the sauce has thickened somewhat.
9. Toss the wings in the sauce until they are uniformly covered.
10. Toss in the peanuts to mix.

2.2 Korean Chicken and Crispy Rice

Cooking Time: 2 hours

Serving Size: 4

Ingredients:

- 4 cups chicken broth
- 6 scallions
- 4 tablespoons unsalted butter
- 2 tablespoons vegetable oil
- 8 chicken drumsticks
- Kosher salt
- ½ teaspoon garlic powder
- ½ teaspoon mustard powder
- 3 cups cooked rice
- 1 teaspoon ground cumin
- 1 tablespoon sesame oil
- 1 teaspoon black pepper
- 2 tablespoons sugar
- 1 tablespoon mirin
- 1 small onion
- ¼ cup gochujang
- ¼ cup soy sauce
- 1 2-inch piece ginger
- 8 garlic cloves

Method:

1. Combine onion, garlic, pepper, gochujang, sour cream, sugar, rice wine, soy sauce, and 1 tablespoon sesame oil in a mixing bowl.
2. Toss together the sauce ingredients in a medium mixing bowl; put aside.
3. In a medium mixing bowl, combine the rice, cumin, garlic powder, and mustard powder; layout on a foil cookie sheet and refrigerate for 1 hour.
4. Meanwhile, season the chicken with salt.
5. Simmer, rotating periodically, for 45–55 minutes, or until poultry is very tender.
6. Cook, occasionally stirring, until the scallions are tender, approximately 3 minutes.
7. Add Salt & pepper to taste.
8. Add 2 thunder thighs and a couple of scallions on top of each cake, with plenty of sauce.

2.3 Spicy Korean Tofu

Cooking Time: 20 minutes

Serving Size: 3

Ingredients:

- 1 tablespoon oil
- 1 box firm tofu

Sauce

- 1 tablespoon sesame oil
- 1/3 cup water
- 1 red chili

- 1 teaspoon white sesame
- 1½ tablespoons red chili power
- 1½ tablespoons soy sauce
- 1 stalk green onion
- 2 cloves garlic
- 1 tablespoon sugar

Method:
1. Divide the tofu into squares with a thickness of approximately ¼ inch.
2. Using paper towels, pat dry.
3. To make the sauce, combine all of the ingredients.
4. Remove from the equation.
5. Heat the oil in a nonstick skillet over medium heat.
6. Reduce the heat to low and add the salsa to the skillet.
7. Boil the tofu until the liquid has thickened but is still a little moist.
8. Flip the tofu over to allow both sides to cook.
9. Serve on a serving dish with chopped scallions on top.
10. Allow cooling before serving.

2.4 Korean Beef Short Ribs

Cooking Time: 7 hours 25 minutes

Serving Size: 5

Ingredients:

- ½ large onion
- 3 pounds short ribs
- 2 tablespoons sesame oil
- ¼ cup minced garlic
- 2 tablespoons white sugar
- 1 tablespoon black pepper
- ¾ cup soy sauce
- 3 tablespoons white vinegar
- ¼ cup dark brown sugar
- ¾ cup water

Method:

1. In a large, non-metallic mixing bowl, combine the soy sauce, wine, and vinegar.
2. Brown honey, coarse flour, pepper, soy sauce, onion, and ginger should be whisked in until the sweets have melted.
3. Cover the ribs with bubble wrap after submerging them in the marinade.
4. Preheat the outside grill to medium-high.
5. Remove the ribs from the marinade, brush off any excess, and discard.

6. Cook 5 to 7 minutes on each side on a hot grill till the flesh is no longer pink.

2.5 Beef Bulgogi

Cooking Time: 1 hour 15 minutes

Serving Size: 4

Ingredients:

- 2 tablespoons sesame oil
- ½ teaspoon black pepper
- 2 tablespoons garlic
- 2 tablespoons sesame seeds
- 1 pound flank steak
- 2 ½ tablespoons white sugar
- ¼ cup green onion
- 5 tablespoons soy sauce

Method:

1. In a small bowl, place the meat. In a small bowl, combine the sesame oil, sugar, fresh basil, garlic, red pepper, soy sauce, and crushed black pepper.
2. Pour the sauce over the meat. Put it in the fridge for at least 1 hour or night, covered.
3. Preheat an outside grill to high heat and brush the grate liberally with oil.
4. 1 to 2 minutes each side on a hot grill, grill meat until slightly browned and cooked through.

2.6 Korean Beef Tacos

Cooking Time: 35 minutes
Serving Size: 12

Ingredients:
Tacos
- 2 tablespoons cilantro leaves
- ¼ teaspoon sesame seeds
- ¼ cup red onion
- 12 mini flour tortillas

Korean Beef
- 2 cloves garlic
- 8 ounces ground beef
- Pinch of ground ginger
- 2 teaspoons vegetable oil
- 1 teaspoon sesame oil
- ¼ teaspoon red-pepper flakes
- 2 tablespoons soy sauce
- 2 tablespoons brown sugar

Sriracha Mayonnaise
- 1 tablespoon Sriracha
- 2 teaspoons lime juice
- ¼ cup mayonnaise

Kimchi
- 1 cup chopped kimchi

- 1 teaspoon sugar
- 2 teaspoons sesame oil

Method:

1. Whisk together cocoa powder, sesame oil, soy sauce, fresh basil, and garlic in a small bowl.
2. In a large skillet, heat the vegetable oil over medium-low heat.
3. Cook, stirring continuously, for 1 minute, or until garlic is aromatic.
4. In a small pan, heat sesame oil over moderate flame.
5. Cook, stirring continuously until the kimchi and sugar are caramelized and cooked through, approximately 3-5 minutes; put aside.
6. Whisk together mayo, Sriracha, and lemon juice in a small bowl; put aside.

2.7 Gochujang Grilled Cheese

Cooking Time: 25 minutes

Serving Size: 2

Ingredients:

Cheese Spread

- 2 tablespoons mayonnaise
- 1 tablespoon red onion
- 2 tablespoons parsley
- 2 tablespoons gochujang
- 2 ounces Gruyère
- 1-ounce fontina cheese
- 2 garlic cloves
- 2 ounces grated white cheddar

Sandwiches and Assembly

- 2 tablespoons olive oil
- 2 tablespoons unsalted butter
- 2 small pickled okra
- ½ cup fresh bean sprouts
- 4 slices Italian bread
- 2 tablespoons mayonnaise
- 2 slices pancetta

Method:

1. To make the cheese spread, follow these steps:

2. In a medium mixing bowl, add Gruyère, white cheese, taleggio cheese, garlic, cilantro, gochujang, mayo, and onions.
3. Over moderate flame, heat a big cast-iron or nonstick pan.
4. Add 2 tablespoons of butter on one side of each piece of bread, total mayo.
5. 2 slices should be turned over, so the mayo side is facing down.
6. Heat the last skillet over medium-high heat.
7. Combine the oil and butter in a mixing bowl, whisk until the butter melts, and then add the sandwiches right away.
8. To melt the cheese well, cover the pan with a lid or a baking sheet; toast until the bread is crusty and brown, 3–5 minutes on each side.
9. Sandwiches should be cut in half and served right away.

2.8 Kimchi

Cooking Time: 30 minutes

Serving Size: 8

Ingredients:

- 2 tablespoons fish sauce
- 2 teaspoons sugar
- 1 shallot, quartered
- 6 tablespoons red pepper flakes
- 1 tablespoon fresh ginger
- 6 cloves garlic, whole
- 2 pounds napa cabbage
- 2 cups daikon radish
- 1 bunch scallions
- ¼ cup sea salt

Method:

1. Save the brine after draining the cabbage.
2. Combine the onion, cloves, onion, red pepper flakes, and fish sauce in a mixing bowl.
3. With tongs or gloves, spread the mixture over the cabbage.
4. Combine the cabbage, onion, and garlic in a big two-quart jar.
5. Cover the jar loosely with a cover to let air escape and set it on a baking dish (or large basin) to catch any liquids that may leak.

2.9 Spicy Radish Salad

Cooking Time: 20 minutes

Serving Size: 4

Ingredients:
- 1-pound Korean radish
- 1 teaspoon sugar
- 1 teaspoon sesame seeds
- ½ teaspoon grated ginger
- 1 tablespoon fish sauce
- 1 teaspoon salt
- 2 tablespoons gochugaru
- 2 teaspoons minced garlic
- 1 or 2 scallions

Method:
1. Toss the radish with the salt and mix well to best fit.
2. Allow about 20 minutes of sitting time, or until the radishes have wilted and given some juice.
3. Remove any surplus liquid. There is no need to rinse.
4. Except for the onion and sesame seeds, combine the other ingredients.
5. By hand, thoroughly combine the ingredients.
6. If required, season with additional salt or fish sauce.
7. Toss everything together, including the onion and sesame seeds.

2.10 Korean Fried Rice

Cooking Time: 50 minutes
Serving Size: 4

Ingredients:

- 150g snow peas
- 3 green shallots
- 1 carrot
- 80g frozen peas
- 2 tablespoon soy sauce
- 2 250g packets rice
- 90g kimchi
- 3 teaspoon fresh ginger
- 2 garlic cloves
- 100g shortcut bacon rashers
- 1 brown onion
- 4 eggs
- 1 ½ tablespoon peanut oil
- 1 tablespoon gochujang
- 1 tablespoon sesame oil
- ½ teaspoon caster sugar

Method:

1. In a small bowl, mix the sesame oil, soya sauce, three tablespoons of sesame oil, and sugar.
2. In a pan, heat two tablespoons of peanut oil on high.

3. Pour in the beaten egg. Scramble until the eggs are almost set.
4. Place on a platter to cool. Clean the wok.
5. Over high heat, cook the remaining peanut oil.
6. Cook bacon in a skillet for 2 minutes, or until brown and crisp combination.
7. Stir-fry for 1-2 minutes, or until the rice is hot and thoroughly mixed.
8. Remove the pan from the heat and add the egg.
9. Shallots should be sprinkled on top.

2.11 Kimchi Soup with Canned Tuna

Cooking Time: 30 minutes
Serving Size: 3

Ingredients:
- 3 cups water
- 185 g canned tuna
- 3 tablespoon water
- ½ cup kimchi

Sauce
- 1 tablespoon Korean chili powder
- ½ tablespoon kimchi juice
- ½ tablespoon Korean fish sauce
- ½ tablespoon raw sugar
- ½ tablespoon soup soy sauce

Method:
1. A medium saucepan should be preheated over a moderate flame (about 20 seconds).

2. Add the cabbage and fish water that has been drained.
3. Stir well until kimchi is almost done (about 2 minutes).
4. Combine the liquid and the sauce in a mixing bowl.
5. Over medium flame, cover the saucepan and bring to a boil.
6. When the water has reached a rolling boil, add the fish and stir gently so that the tuna does not break apart.
7. Turn down the heat to low, cover the pot, and cook for another 15-20 minutes.

2.12 Yukgaejang (Spicy Beef Soup)

Cooking Time: 2 hours 20 minutes
Serving Size: 4

Ingredients:
Main

- 2 tablespoon Korean chili oils
- 200g bean sprouts
- 95 g shiitake mushrooms
- 100g hydrated gosari
- 1 tablespoon cooking oil
- 75g green onion
- 3 tablespoon Korean chili powder
- 3 tablespoon sesame oil

Beef Broth

- 75g green onions
- 1 teaspoon black peppercorn
- 350g beef brisket
- 1 onion
- 10 cups water

Seasonings

- ½ teaspoon fine sea salt
- 1/8 teaspoon ground black pepper
- 1 tablespoon Korean fish sauce
- ½ tablespoon minced garlic

- 2 tablespoon Korean soup soy sauce

Method:

1. To pull out the crimson liquid (myoglobin), immerse the beef in a basin of water for 20 minutes.
2. Cover and cook with the top and lower the heat to moderate low after the water begins to boil.
3. Place the meat on a dish and set it aside to cool.
4. Preheat a big clean saucepan over low heat, then add the cooking oil, sesame oil, green onions and whisk to combine.
5. Add the chili powder after the green onions have wilted and stir for approximately 30 seconds, just until the dried chilies have absorbed all of the oils.
6. In a large saucepan, combine the broth, the beef, and the shiitake mushrooms, and bring to a boil over medium flame.
7. Boil for another 10 minutes after adding the bean sprouts.

2.13 Korean Spicy Squid Rice Bowl (Ojingeo Deopbap)

Cooking Time: 25 minutes

Serving Size: 2

Ingredients:

- 2 cups cooked rice
- Fried egg
- Some cooking oils
- 1 teaspoon sesame oil

- 270g squid
- 50g carrot
- 60g onion
- 20g green onion
- 80g cabbage
- 1 tablespoon rice wine

Seasoning Sauce

- 1 teaspoon minced garlic
- Ground black pepper
- 2.5 tablespoon Korean chili oil
- 1 tablespoon sugar
- 1.5 tablespoon soy sauce
- 2 tablespoon gochugaru
- 1 tablespoon gochujang

Method:

1. In a mixing saucepan, place the calamari rings.
2. Stir in the rice wine completely.
3. In a dish, combine all of the seasoning sauce ingredients and put them aside.
4. Preheat a saucepan over medium heat until it is completely hot.
5. Combine the remaining veggies in the pot.
6. Stir constantly over medium-high heat till the lettuce has wilted somewhat (about 2 minutes).
7. Combine the calamari and the spice sauce in a mixing bowl.
8. In a large mixing bowl, combine the veggies and stir well.

9. Turn off the heat.

10. Add the soy sauce and immediately mix it in.

11. Serve the squid and veggies over rice in a dish.

2.14 Grilled Gochujang Chicken Recipe

Cooking Time: 4 hours

Serving Size: 2

Ingredients:

- 100g Korean rice cakes
- Cooking oil
- 100g sweet potato
- 450g boneless thigh fillets

Gochujang Chicken Marinade

- 2 teaspoon ginger
- A few black peppers
- ¼ cup Sprite
- 2 teaspoon soy sauce
- 2 teaspoon garlic
- 1 tablespoon brown sugar
- 1 tablespoon onion powder
- ½ tablespoon gochugaru
- 1 tablespoon rice wine (mirin)
- 3 tablespoon gochujang

Method:

1. Cook the chicken depending on the kind of grill you have and your preferences.
2. In a mixing dish, combine all of the leftover marinades and stir thoroughly.
3. Over the chicken, pour the sauce.

4. To uniformly coat the poultry with the sauce, combine all of the ingredients in a mixing bowl.
5. To enhance the taste, cover and marinate it for at least three hours or night in the refrigerator.
6. Grease the grill pan and heat the barbecue according to the manufacturer's instructions.

2.15 Japchae (Korean Glass Noodle Stir Fry)

Cooking Time: 55 minutes

Serving Size: 8

Ingredients:

Spinach Seasoning

- ½ teaspoon minced garlic
- 1 teaspoon toasted sesame oil
- ¼ teaspoon fine sea salt
- 1 garlic
- 1 tablespoon soy sauce

Other

- ½ yellow onion
- 100g fresh shiitake mushroom
- 110g baby spinach
- ¼ red capsicum
- 100g rib eye fillet
- 1 carrot
- 250g Korean starch noodles

Beef Marinade

- ¼ teaspoon ground black pepper
- 1 teaspoon toasted sesame oil
- 1 teaspoon rice wine (mirin)
- ½ teaspoon minced

Noodles & Mushroom Marinade

- 1 tablespoon toasted sesame oil
- 1/8 teaspoon ground black pepper
- 1 tablespoon honey
- 1 tablespoon brown sugar
- 4 tablespoon soy sauce

Method:
1. In a medium mixing dish, place the beef strips.
2. Add the meat, marinate to the meat, and gently fold it in.
3. Boil the greens in a pot of boiling water for a few minutes.
4. Stir in the spinach flavor in a gentle and equal manner.
5. Pour the remainder of the noodles and mushroom marinated sauce into a flour mixture with the pasta.
6. With a spoon, beat the uncooked egg.
7. Pour in the egg white solution and cook over low heat on both sides (1-2 minutes).
8. It should be placed in the big mixing basin.
9. Over medium heat, soften the veggies, pork, and scallops with a touch of salt (1-2 minutes).

Chapter 3: Korean Dinner Recipes

3.1 Noodles with Chilled Tomato Broth

Cooking Time: 35 minutes
Serving Size: 4

Ingredients:
- ½ cup cilantro leaves
- Hot chili paste
- ½ tablespoon unsalted butter
- 2 medium Persian cucumbers
- 10 oz. thin noodles
- 5 large eggs
- 1½ lb. tomatoes
- 1 tablespoon sugar
- 1 tablespoon kosher salt
- 3 tablespoon rice vinegar
- 1 small garlic clove

Method:
1. In a blender, combine tomato, garlic, balsamic, honey, salt, and 2 cups of liquid at low speed.
2. Meanwhile, prepare the noodles as per package instructions in a large pot of hot simmering water.
3. Salt and pepper the beaten eggs.
4. In a large skillet over medium heat, melt butter over low heat.
5. Swirl half of the beaten eggs around the skillet to create a thin egg crepe.

6. Distribute the noodles among the bowls.
7. Pour tomatoes broth over the top, skimming off any froth.
8. In bowls, layer shredded eggs, cucumbers, onions, and cilantro.
9. Serve with a side of spicy chili paste.

3.2 Kimchi Udon with Scallions

Cooking Time: 20 minutes
Serving Size: 4

Ingredients:
- 3 scallions
- 1 tablespoon sesame seeds
- Kosher salt
- 4 large egg yolks
- ½ cup chicken broth
- 1 pound udon noodles
- 1 cup kimchi
- 2 tablespoons gochujang
- 5 tablespoons unsalted butter

Method:
1. In a large pan, melt 2 tablespoons of butter over moderate flame.
2. Cook, turning periodically, with the chopped kimchi and gochujang.
3. Bring the broth and cabbage juice to a low simmer.
4. Cook for three minutes or until liquid is somewhat reduced.
5. Next, boil the noodles as directed on the box.
6. Transfer the noodles to the pan with tongs and add the butter; cook, often turning, until the sauce covers the noodles, approximately 2 minutes.

7. If necessary, season with salt.

3.3 Grilled Chili-Lemongrass Short Ribs with Pickled Daikon

Cooking Time: 1 hour

Serving Size: 4

Ingredients:

- Kosher salt
- 6 oz. daikon
- 5 tablespoon seasoned rice vinegar
- 3 lb. beef ribs
- 1 teaspoon toasted sesame oil
- ¼ cup vegetable oil
- 4 red Fresno
- 3 garlic cloves
- 1 tablespoon light brown sugar
- 1 ginger
- 3 lemongrass stalks

Method:

1. In a food processor, puree the chilis, lemongrass, garlic, ginger, black pepper, sesame oil, ¼ cup sunflower oil, and vinegar until clear.
2. Place the ribs in a glass baking dish and season both sides with salt.
3. Pour the chili paste over the ribs and flip them to coat them.

4. Allow for at least a few minutes and up to 1 hour at ambient temperature.
5. Heat a grill to high temperatures.
6. Allow five minutes for resting on a plate.
7. To serve, sprinkle daikon over the ribs and pour any remaining liquid into the dish.

3.4 Tteokguk (Good Luck Cake Soup)

Cooking Time: 50 minutes
Serving Size: 4

Ingredients:
- Freshly ground black pepper
- Korean red chili threads
- 10 ounces Korean rice cakes
- 2 teaspoons fish sauce
- 1/3 Korean radish
- 4 large eggs
- 4 scallions
- 1 tablespoon vegetable oil
- Kosher salt
- 1 piece ginger
- 1 ½-pound beef brisket
- 1 teaspoon sesame oil
- 4 garlic cloves

Method:
1. In a large saucepan over medium-high heat, temperature sesame oil, and vegetable oil. Sprinkle with salt.

2. Cook for about 15 minutes, flipping once.
3. Smash the ginger in a small bowl.
4. Using a slotted spoon, transfer the meat to a dish and discard the ginger and scallion whites.
5. Simmer the Korean radish.
6. Cook the eggs for approximately 2 minutes, stirring occasionally.
7. Return the meat to the saucepan, thinly sliced, and add the rice cakes.
8. Place sliced egg, saved scallion leaves, and chili strands on top of the soup in dishes.

3.5 Gochujang with Scallion Grilled Chicken Wings

Cooking Time: 30 minutes

Serving Size: 4

Ingredients:

- ½ cup gochujang
- 1 scallion
- 1 teaspoon kosher salt
- ½ teaspoon black pepper
- 1 tablespoon vegetable oil
- 2 pounds chicken wings

Method:

1. Using paper towels, pat the wings extremely dry. In a large mixing basin, toss the wings with the oil, salt, and pepper.

2. Prepare a grill with two zones, followed by medium heat, or heat a grilling skillet over medium heat.
3. Over medium heat, cook wings in batches.
4. In a large mixing basin, combine the red curry paste and ¼ cup boiling water.
5. Toss the wings in the gochujang-coated basin. Place on a serving tray.

3.6 Instant-Pot Kimchi Coleslaw and Korean Chili-Braised Brisket

Cooking Time: 3 hours 30 minutes

Serving Size: 8

Ingredients:

- Two teaspoons Asian fish sauce
- 1 teaspoon sesame oil
- 2 tablespoons soy sauce
- 2 tablespoons light brown sugar
- ¼ cup gochujang
- 2 tablespoons ketchup
- 1 tablespoon fresh ginger
- 1 cup lager-style beer
- 5 pounds beef brisket
- 1 large onion
- 4 garlic cloves
- ½ teaspoon black pepper
- 3 tablespoons peanut oil

- 1 tablespoon sweet paprika
- 2½ teaspoons kosher salt
- 1 tablespoon red chili flakes

Kimchi Coleslaw

- Juice of ½ lime
- ½ teaspoon fine sea salt
- 2 tablespoons peanut oil
- 1 teaspoon sesame oil
- ¼ cup kimchi
- 5 cups cabbage

Method:

1. Chili peppers, paprika, garlic, and pepper are rubbed into the meat.
2. Put it in the fridge for 1 hour or up to an hour after covering.
3. Add a teaspoon of oil, wait a few minutes for it to heat up, then pour a batch of beef and broil until it's browned all over.
4. Add onion and cook for five minutes, or until golden.
5. Sauté for a further minute after adding the garlic and ginger.
6. Combine the beer, gochujang, vinegar, soy sauce, coconut milk, shrimp paste, and sesame oil in a large mixing bowl.
7. Cover and cook for 90 minutes on high pressure.
8. In a large mixing basin, toss together the lettuce, kimchi, oils, lemon juice, and salt to create the kimchi coleslaw.

9. If necessary, season with additional salt or lime juice.

3.7 Gochujang-Braised Chicken and Crispy Rice

Cooking Time: 1 hour
Serving Size: 4

Ingredients:

- 4 cups chicken broth
- 6 scallions
- 4 tablespoons unsalted butter
- 2 tablespoons vegetable oil
- 8 chicken drumsticks
- Kosher salt
- ½ teaspoon garlic powder
- ½ teaspoon mustard powder
- 3 cups cooked rice
- 1 teaspoon ground cumin
- 1 tablespoon sesame oil
- 1 teaspoon black pepper
- 1 small onion
- 2 tablespoons sugar
- 1 tablespoon mirin
- 8 garlic cloves
- ¼ cup gochujang
- ¼ cup soy sauce

- 1 (2-inch) piece ginger

Method:
1. In a medium mixing bowl, add onion, clove, spice, sriracha, sesame oil, sugar, mirin, soy sauce, and pepper; put aside.
2. In a medium mixing bowl, add the rice, cumin, red pepper, and tamarind paste.
3. Meanwhile, liberally season the chicken with salt.
4. Cook, rotating periodically until chicken is gently browned, approximately 5 minutes.
5. Divide the rice into four equal pieces.
6. Over medium heat, heat a large microwaveable bowl.
7. Cook rice cakes in two batches, rotating halfway through, for approximately 10 minutes, until crispy, puffy, and golden.

3.8 Spicy Korean Steak Tacos with Kimchi

Cooking Time: 1 hour

Serving Size: 16

Ingredients:

Spicy Ginger Sauce

- 1 teaspoon dried chili flakes
- 1 tablespoon sugar
- 1 tablespoon cooking wine
- 1 tablespoon ginger
- 2 tablespoons oyster sauce

For the Tacos

- 1 cup kimchi
- ½ cup coriander
- ½ cup Japanese mayonnaise
- 2 cups daikon
- 16 small flour tortillas

Method:

1. Add a few drops of oil to the steaks.
2. Cover a plate with half of the rock salt, top with the fillets and the rest of the salt. Allow twenty minutes to pass.
3. Using a paper towel, remove any salt from the cuts and season with pepper.
4. Prepare a griddle pan or a grill on high.
5. Cook the steak for 2–3 minutes per side, or until done to your satisfaction, flipping every minute.

3.9 Korean-Style Grain Bowls with Spicy Marinated Steak

Cooking Time: 1 hour 45 minutes

Serving Size: 4

Ingredients:

For the Marinade

- 1 teaspoon sugar
- ¼ teaspoon kosher salt
- 1 tablespoon ginger
- 1 teaspoon gochujang
- 1 cup pear juice

- 3 garlic cloves
- 2 tablespoons sesame oil
- ½ cup rice wine vinegar
- ¼ cup vegetable oil
- ½ cup soy sauce

Grain Bowls

- 2 teaspoons toasted sesame seeds
- Gochujang
- 4 fried eggs
- 1 scallion
- 6 ounces sugar snap peas
- ½ cup kimchi
- 1½ cups purple cabbage
- 4 cups cooked grains
- ½ teaspoon kosher salt
- 1 large carrot
- 4 cups baby spinach
- 2 tablespoons rice wine vinegar

For the Beef

- 1 ½ pound short ribs
- 1 tablespoon vegetable oil
- 1 teaspoon light brown sugar
- ½ teaspoon kosher salt
- 2 teaspoons gochujang

Method:

1. In a medium mixing bowl, combine the pears, soy sauce, wine, sunflower oil, garlic, soy sauce, ginger, sriracha, coconut milk, and salt.
2. Reserve the leftover marinade in a large plastic baggie or dish.
3. Gochujang, black pepper, and salt are whisked together.
4. Allow for at least 1 hour of resting time after adding the steak and tossing it to coat it.
5. Over medium-high heat, heat the oil in a large pan.
6. For a medium-rare steak, cook 2–3 minutes on each side.

3.10 Spicy Kimchi Tofu Stew

Cooking Time: 40 minutes

Serving Size: 4

Ingredients:

- 6 large egg yolks
- 2 tablespoons sesame seeds
- 1 tablespoon sesame oil
- Freshly ground black pepper
- 8 scallions
- 2 tablespoons soy sauce
- 4 cups cabbage kimchi
- 2 tablespoons gochujang
- 1 16-ounce silken tofu
- 1 tablespoon vegetable oil

- Kosher salt

Method:

1. A big saucepan of salted water should be brought to a boil.
2. Reduce heat to low, add tofu, and slowly simmer.
3. In a big heavy saucepan, heat cooking oil over moderate flame.
4. Cook, often turning, until the cabbage and gochujang begin to color, 5–8 minutes.
5. Bring to a boil, lower to low heat, cook for 35–40 minutes, or until the kimchi is soft and transparent.
6. Simmer gently with the onions, miso, and tofu.
7. Season with salt & chili, and sesame oil.

3.11 Beef Short Ribs Satay (Satay Kra-Toog Ngua)

Cooking Time:

Serving Size: 4

Ingredients:

Marinade

- 1/3 cup coconut milk
- 1 pound beef short ribs
- 1 tablespoon fish sauce
- ¼ teaspoon turmeric power
- 2 tablespoons canola oil
- 2 tablespoons oyster sauce
- ¼ cup lemongrass
- ¼ cup shallots
- 5 garlic cloves
- 1/8 cup fresh ginger

For the Baste

- Kosher salt, to taste
- 1/3 cup coconut milk

Method:

1. Put the lemon, garlic, onions, and cloves in a mortar and crush a semi-smooth pulp.
2. In a large mixing bowl, combine the oil, sesame oil, shrimp paste, turmeric, and ¼ cup peanut butter.

3. Preheat your grill to high heat when it's time to prepare the ribs.
4. To make the baste, combine the ¼ cup marinade and 1/3 cup coconut milk in a mixing bowl.
5. On each side, grill the ribs for approximately 2 minutes.

3.12 Spring Bibimbap

Cooking Time: 45 minutes

Serving Size: 2

Ingredients:

- 1 avocado
- Gochujang
- 2 cups Napa Cabbage
- Kimchi
- 5 cups cooked rice
- 2 squares toasted nori
- 1–2 teaspoons sesame oil
- 1 tablespoon black sesame seeds
- 2 bunches of Swiss chard
- 2 teaspoons rice vinegar
- 2 tablespoons oil
- 1 tablespoon sugar
- ¾ teaspoon fine sea salt
- 1 medium carrot
- 6 small radishes
- 1 big Kirby cucumber

Method:

1. Combine the veggies and chard stems in a mixing dish.
2. Toss the vegetables with the honey and ¾ teaspoon of salt, then rinse and drain.

3. Meantime, heat one tablespoon impartial oil in a pan over medium heat.
4. Cook, stirring regularly with tongs, for five minutes, adding the Swiss chard stems in increments.
5. In a large skillet, heat and cook one tablespoon oil and one teaspoon garlic powder just before serving.
6. Make a thick cake out of the rice in the skillet.
7. To serve, scoop out the rice with a spatula and distribute this among four bowls.
8. Swiss spinach, sriracha, and avocado are served on top.

3.13 Butter Mandu (Butter Dumplings)

Cooking Time: 1 hour 10 minutes
Serving Size: 6

Ingredients:

- Light soy sauce
- Vegetable or sesame oil
- 45 Asian dumpling wrappers
- 1 tablespoon kosher salt
- 1 pound butter
- 4 garlic cloves
- 2 pounds ground pork
- 2 cups green cabbage
- 2-inch knob of ginger
- Fresh Napa Cabbage

Method:

1. In the mixing bowl, pulse the lettuce, carrot, and garlic until thinly sliced.
2. In a large mixing basin, combine the cabbage and other vegetables.
3. Place approximately two teaspoons of the mixture in the middle of each wrapper to construct the mandu.
4. Glaze the border of the wrapper with your fingers dipped in a glass of water.
5. To cover the wrapper, fold it in half to create a half-moon and squeeze the ends together.

3.14 Bo Ssäm Grilled Pork and Pickled Slaw in Lettuce Cups

Cooking Time: 1 hour 30 minutes

Serving Size: 4

> **Ingredients:**
> **Radishes and Carrots**
> - 6 radishes
> - 2 carrots
> - 4 teaspoons kosher salt
> - ½ teaspoon black pepper
> - ¼ cup sugar
> - ½ cup rice wine vinegar
>
> **Wraps**
> - 3 cups cooked rice
> - Sriracha hot sauce
> - 2 heads Boston
> - 2 scallions
> - 2 pounds BBQ pork butt

Method:
1. Mix vinegar, honey, pepper, spice, and ½ cup water in a medium mixing bowl.
2. Allow radish and vegetables to sit for at least ten minutes before serving.
3. Preheat the oven to 250 degrees Fahrenheit.

4. Pour a few tablespoons of water into a baking dish with the pork.

5. Wrap in foil and reheat the pork for 20–25 minutes, or until hot.

3.15 Mochi-Covered Strawberries

Cooking Time: 43 minutes

Serving Size: 6

Ingredients:

- 2 tablespoon sugar
- ¾ cup water
- 1 ½ tablespoon sugar
- ⅔ cup water
- 6 strawberries
- Potato starch/cornstarch
- 100g Shiratamako Package
- 5.3 oz red bean paste

Method:

1. Strawberries should be rinsed, dried, and hulled.
2. Anko should be divided into 6 equal-sized balls.
3. Anko should be used to wrap the strawberries.
4. Whisk together shiratamako and sugar in a medium microwave-safe glass bowl.
5. Slowly add water in three parts, constantly stirring, until the mixture reaches a powdery texture.
6. Place the mochi on top of the corn starch on the tray.

7. Begin by wrapping the strawberry from across all sides and holding the mochi in place with your thumb.
8. Twist and close the mochi if all sides meet at the bottom.

Chapter 4: Korean Snacks and Dessert Recipes

4.1 Korean Coleslaw

Cooking Time: 15 minutes

Serving Size: 6

Ingredients:

- Salt, to taste
- Pepper, to taste
- 1 tablespoon sesame oil
- 1 tablespoon sesame seeds
- 2 tablespoons sugar
- 2 tablespoons red pepper
- 2 tablespoons soy sauce
- 2 tablespoons rice vinegar
- 1 small head green cabbage
- 5 scallions
- 3 cloves garlic
- 1 carrot
- 1 sweet onion
- 1 cup red cabbage

Method:

1. In a large mixing basin, mix the lettuce, carrots, ginger, and onions.

2. In a small mixing bowl, combine the onion, sesame oil, balsamic, sweetener, red pepper, soy sauce, and black pepper.

3. Toss the veggies with the dressing to coat them.

4. Season to taste, then season with salt and pepper if necessary.

5. Serve right away or set aside for a few hours to let the flavors meld.

4.2 Korean Egg Bread

Cooking Time: 50 minutes

Serving Size: 8

Ingredients:

- Pinch fine sea salt
- Some melted butter
- ¼ teaspoon vanilla essence
- 6 small eggs
- 1/3 cup milk
- 1/3 cup melted salted butter
- ¼ teaspoon ground salt
- 1 large egg (for batter)
- 1/3 cup castor sugar
- 2/3 cup self-rising flour

Method:

1. Preheat the oven to 180°C for 20 minutes.
2. Brush the tiny muffin holes on the pan with melted butter.
3. In a large mixing bowl, sift together the flour, sugar, and salt.
4. In a small dish, mix one egg, water, margarine, and vanilla extract.
5. In a large mixing basin, combine two and three above and well combine.
6. Scoop a portion of the batter into the muffin tin.

7. Bake for 25 minutes with the muffin pan in the oven.
8. Allow 3-4 minutes for the tray to cool.

4.3 Korean Popcorn Chicken

Cooking Time: 1 hour 5 minutes
Serving Size: 3

Ingredients:

- 1 cup potato starch
- Some cooking oil
- ½ teaspoon fine sea salt
- ¼ teaspoon ground black pepper
- 500g chicken thigh fillets
- 1 tablespoon rice wine
- 2 teaspoon ginger powder
- 150g fresh Korean rice cake

Sauce

- 2 teaspoon sesame oil
- ½ teaspoon minced garlic
- 2 tablespoon dark brown sugar
- 1 tablespoon soy sauce
- 1 ½ tablespoon gochujang
- 2 tablespoon honey
- 5 tablespoon tomato sauce

Method:

1. In a large mixing bowl, place the chicken chunks.
2. Mix in the white wine, garlic powder, seasoning, and freshly ground smoked paprika.

3. Thoroughly cover each chicken piece in the starch powder.
4. In a deep sauté pan, heat some vegetable oil till it reaches 175 degrees Celsius.
5. In batches, deep-fry the baked potatoes until the outside layer becomes crispy.
6. In a hot skillet, pour the sauce.
7. Bring to a boil over medium heat, occasionally stirring, until the mixture thickens slightly. Constantly stir.
8. Add the cooked chicken and rice cakes, then quickly and completely cover them in the sauce.

4.4 Korean Mochi Doughnut Holes

Cooking Time: 1 hour 40 minutes
Serving Size: 32

Ingredients:
Dough

- ¼ teaspoon fine sea salt
- 500ml hot milk
- 80g self-rising flour
- 20g melted butter
- 500 g sweet rice flour

Stuffing

- 220 g Nutella

Others

- 50g castor sugar
- ½ teaspoon cinnamon powder
- Vegetable oil

Method:

1. In a large mixing basin, combine self-rising flour and baking powder.
2. Combine the melted butter and salt in a mixing bowl.
3. Slowly pour in the heated milk.
4. To create tiny round balls, pour the mixture onto a work surface and divide it into tiny chunks.
5. Seal the dough with a tablespoon of Nutella.

6. In a deep saucepan, pour some frying oil and cook it for 6 to 8 minutes.
7. Gently press the donut holes into the dough.
8. Combine the sugar and cardamom powder in a medium or large food-grade plastic bag.
9. Carry on with the remaining doughnut holes in the same manner. Serve.

4.5 Sweet Pancake

Cooking Time: 30 minutes

Serving Size: 4

Ingredients:

- 4 tablespoons unsalted butter
- 1 teaspoon vanilla extract
- 1¼ cups milk
- 1 large egg
- 1 tablespoon baking powder
- ½ teaspoon of fine sea
- 2 tablespoons sugar
- 1 ½ cups all-purpose flour

Method:

1. In a medium mixing basin, combine the flour, sugar, baking powder, and salt.
2. Combine the milk, egg, softened butter, and vanilla essence in a mixing bowl.
3. Over moderate flame, heat, and cook.
4. Using melted butter, lightly coat the skillet.
5. Spoon mixture into skillet using a ¼-cup measuring cup.
6. Turn the pancake over when the edges seem dry and bubble form and burst on the upper surface.

4.6 Korean Fish Cake Soup

Cooking Time: 35 minutes

Serving Size: 2

Ingredients:
- A few sprinkles of black pepper
- Fine sea salt
- 1 tablespoon rice wine
- 1 teaspoon minced garlic
- 30g green onion
- 1 tablespoon soy sauce
- 200g Korean fish cakes

Broth
- 30g dried anchovy
- 100g white radish
- 10g dried kelp
- 6 cups water

Method:
1. In a medium/large saucepan, combine the water, dried kelp, and anchovies.
2. Cook for 10 minutes over medium heat, uncovered.
3. Cook for another 10 minutes with the radish and anchovies.
4. Using a sharp knife, cut the roast potatoes into tiny rectangles.
5. Bring the broth and radish to a boil on medium-high heat, then add the sesame oil, rice wine, and garlic.

6. Stir for a few seconds.
7. Turn down the heat to moderate after the water has boiled.
8. Add the fritters to the soup and cook until they are mushy and have absorbed the soup's flavor.

4.7 Tteokbokki

Cooking Time: 20 minutes

Serving Size: 2

Ingredients:
- 2 cups soup stock
- 60g onion
- 150g Korean fish cakes
- 350g Korean rice cakes

Tteokbokki Sauce
- 1 teaspoon garlic
- 1 teaspoon gochugaru
- 1½ tablespoon raw sugar
- 1 tablespoon soy sauce
- 3 tablespoon gochujang

Garnish
- 1 teaspoon sesame seeds
- 1 teaspoon sesame oil
- 1 stalk green onion

Method:
1. Soak your rice cakes in warm water for a few minutes unless they're already soft.

2. In a small saucepan over medium-high heat, bring the soup stock to a boil, then whisk in the tteokbokki sauce with a spatula to dissolve it.

3. Add the baked potatoes, fish cakes, and onion to the seasoned boiling stock.

4. Cook for 3 to 5 minutes more, or until the oatmeal cookies are completely cooked.

5. Then, to thicken the sauces and enhance the taste, cook it for another 2 to 4 minutes over low heat.

6. Quickly whisk in the sesame oil, red pepper, and fresh basil.

7. Warm the dish before serving.

4.8 Easy Baked Yagkwa

Cooking Time: 3 hours 55 minutes

Serving Size: 20

Ingredients:

For the Cookie Dough

- ¼ cup's sake
- ¼ cup water
- ¼ cup sesame oil
- ¼ cup honey
- 3 cups flour

For the Syrup

- 1 cup honey
- 1 small piece of ginger
- ½ cup rice malt syrup

Other
- ¼ cup pine nuts
- 1 tablespoon sesame seeds
- 3 cups vegetable oil

Method:
1. In a large mixing bowl, sift the flour.
2. Mix in the sesame oil by hand, kneading the flour with your palms and fingers to fully incorporate it.
3. Whisk together the syrup, wine, and water in a small dish.
4. To make a dough, add the liquid components to the egg mixture and mix gently with your hands.
5. In a medium saucepan, combine the rice peach puree, honey, and ginger.
6. Bring to a low simmer, then remove from the heat.
7. Heat over moderate flame until the oil reaches 212 degrees Fahrenheit.
8. Drop pastries into oil in small batches and fry, gently rotating them till they puff up and float, approximately 4 to 5 minutes.
9. Once all of the yakka has been put in the syrup, flip them over once more to ensure that they are evenly covered.
10. Soak for 2 to 3 hours in the syrup.
11. Using a slotted spoon, transfer to a new dish lined with paper towels.

4.9 Hotteok (Korean Sweet Pancakes)

Cooking Time: 1 hour 50 minutes
Serving Size: 6

Ingredients:

- ½ cup lukewarm milk
- cooking oil
- 1 teaspoon white sugar
- 1 teaspoon instant dry yeast
- ½ teaspoon fine sea salt
- 1¼ cup all-purpose flour

Fillings

- ¼ teaspoon cinnamon powder
- 2 tablespoon crushed nuts
- ¼ cup dark brown sugar

Method:

1. In a large mixing bowl, sieve the flour, then add a pinch of salt, sugars, fermentation, and milk.
2. Cover the basin with plastic wrap after thoroughly mixing them into a dough.
3. Cover again with the wrap and set aside for another 20 minutes.
4. Place one of the dough pieces in your palm and flatten it with your fingers so how you can add approximately 1 tablespoon of filling.
5. Preheat a deep fryer on medium heat a thin coating of cooking oil once it's hot.
6. Cook a dough ball in the skillet over medium heat until the underside is gently golden brown.

7. Cook till golden brown on the bottom.
8. Place the pancake on a dish and set it aside.

4.10 Paleo Songpyeon Recipe

Cooking Time: 30 minutes

Serving Size: 20

Ingredients:

Songpyeon Wrapper

- 2 large eggs
- 1 tablespoon rice vinegar
- ¼ cup tapioca starch
- 1/8 teaspoon sea salt
- ½ cup almond flour
- 1¼ cup cassava flour

Other ingredients

- Sesame oil
- Coldwater

Sweet Sesame Filling

- 1 tablespoon coconut sugar
- 1/8 teaspoon sea salt
- 2 tablespoons honey
- ½ cup sesame seeds

For Green Dough

- Water as needed
- 4 teaspoon matcha powder

For Yellow Dough

- 2 teaspoon turmeric powder

- Water as needed

For White Dough

- Water as needed

For Pink Dough

- Water as needed
- 2 tablespoon pureed beets

Method:

1. To make the wrapper dough, combine all of the ingredients in a mixing dish and mix with a whisk until crumbled.
2. In a food processor, combine all filling ingredients and pulse several times until the sweet potatoes are broken down and aromatic.
3. Toss in approximately ½ teaspoon of sesame filling.
4. To cover the filling, fold the bread in half.
5. Over medium-high heat, bring the mixture to a boil.
6. Fill the steamer basket halfway with songpyeon.
7. Steam for three minutes with the lid on.

Chapter 5: Vegetarian Korean Recipes

5.1 Minari

Cooking Time: 15 minutes

Serving Size: 6

Ingredients:

- 2 teaspoon sesame oil
- 2 teaspoon toasted sesame seeds
- 2 teaspoons sugar
- 1 tablespoon Korean plum extract
- 1 bunch minari
- 1 tablespoon rice vinegar
- 1 clove garlic
- ¼ large onion
- 2 tablespoon soy sauce
- 1 tablespoon anchovy sauce
- 1 tablespoon chili flakes
- 1½ tablespoon chili paste

Method:

1. Put sugar, anchovy sauce, chili paste, soy sauce, chili flakes, garlic, rice vinegar, and toasted sesame seeds in a large serving bowl and stir well.
2. Minari and onion should be added at this point.
3. Toss gently with the fingers to evenly coat the minari with the balsamic dressing.

5.2 Broccoli with Tofu

Cooking Time: 55 minutes

Serving Size: 4

Ingredients:

- 1 tablespoon cornstarch
- 1½ teaspoon sesame seeds
- 2 tablespoons agave syrup
- 1 tablespoon rice vinegar
- 1 teaspoon ginger
- ¼ cup soy sauce
- 3 tablespoons vegetable broth
- 2 garlic cloves
- 14 oz firm tofu
- 1 ½ teaspoon sesame oil
- 3 cups broccoli florets
- 1 teaspoon vegetable oil

Method:

1. Place the tofu on a dish wrapped in two layers of towels.
2. Heat the sunflower oil and 1 teaspoon olive oil in a large Teflon skillet over medium heat.
3. Combine the broccoli and vegetable broth in a heated pan.
4. Turn down the heat to intermediate and cover.

5. Add the remaining 12 teaspoons of sesame oil, as well as the garlic and ginger. Stir until the mixture has softened.
6. Combine the sesame oil, agave nectar, rice vinegar, and starch slurry in a mixing bowl.
7. Stir until the mixture has thickened to the desired consistency.
8. Toss the tofu in the sauce and return it to the pan.

5.3 Crunchy Nut Candy

Cooking Time: 15 minutes

Serving Size: 7

Ingredients:

- 2 cups miniature marshmallows
- 3 cups crisp rice cereal
- 1 cup chunky peanut butter
- 2 cups peanuts
- 1 package white candy coating

Method:

1. Melt candy topping in a microwave-safe dish.
2. Add the peanut butter and mix well.
3. Combine the remaining ingredients and fold them in.
4. Using a tablespoon, drop onto plastic wrap.
5. Chill until ready to use.

5.4 Stir-Fried Oyster Mushrooms

Cooking Time: 15 minutes
Serving Size: 4

Ingredients:
- ¼ teaspoon Szechuan peppercorn
- Coriander stems optional
- 6 green onions
- 2 tablespoon cooking oil
- 1 teaspoon dark soy sauce
- 1 thumb ginger
- 1.5 tablespoon oyster sauce
- 400g oyster mushroom

Method:
1. Heat the oil over medium heat in a wok and cook the green leaf whites and carrot pieces until fragrant.
2. Put the mushrooms in the pot.
3. Combine the oyster sauce and black soy sauce in a mixing bowl.
4. The procedure should take 1 to 2 minutes or until the mushrooms have darkened significantly.
5. Sichuan peppercorn flour or powdered black pepper may be used.
6. Sections of green onion should be added.

5.5 Seasoned Seaweed

Cooking Time: 10 minutes

Serving Size: 4

Ingredients:

- 3 tablespoon sesame oil
- 2 tablespoon sesame seeds
- 3 tablespoon soy sauce
- 1 tablespoon sugar
- 3 garlic
- 3 green onions
- 100g Doljaban

Method:

1. Add minced garlic, fresh basil, three tablespoons sesame oil, 1/3 cup liquid, sugar or syrup, and three tablespoons olive oil to a large serving bowl and stir thoroughly with a spoon.
2. With both hands, tear or smash the doljaban into tiny pieces and put it in the bowl with the seasoning sauce.
3. Mix well until all of the moisture has been absorbed.
4. Toss in some toasted sesame seeds and combine everything.
5. Serve alongside rice, kimchi, broth, and a few other sides.

5.6 Sweet and Crunchy Tofu

Cooking Time: 40 minutes

Serving Size: 4

Ingredients:

- 1 tablespoon pumpkin seeds
- Cooked white rice
- ¼ cup Korean rice syrup
- 3 tablespoons gochujang
- 2 cups vegetable oil
- ¼ cup ketchup
- ¼ cup potato starch
- 14 ounces firm tofu

Method:

1. Place the tofu squares in a strap bag and slice into 1-inch dice.
2. Pour the potato starch, cover the container, and flip it over gently until all the tofu is covered.
3. Add the oil to 340 degrees in a big, deep pan or Dutch oven over moderate flame.
4. Cook for 10 to 15 minutes, carefully adds the tofu pieces a few at a time.
5. Mix the ketchup, rice sugar, and gochujang in a big skillet (ideally nonstick) over medium-high temperature.
6. Cook, constantly stirring, for 1 to 2 minutes, or until the sauce bubbles.
7. Reheat the sauce until it is boiling over medium-high heat.

8. Toss in the heated fried tofu gently to coat.

5.7 Healthy Vegetable Rice Bowl

Cooking Time: 25 minutes

Serving Size: 2

Ingredients:
- Sprinkle of sesame seeds
- ½ avocado
- ¼ cup fresh basil
- ¼ cup toasted peanuts
- ½ cup cooked black beans
- 2 tablespoons pickled ginger
- 2 handfuls snap peas
- ½ English cucumber
- 2 cups green cabbage
- 1 small carrot
- 2 cups cooked rice
- 1 small ripe ataulfo mango

Dressing
- 2 teaspoons cane sugar
- ½ teaspoon sriracha
- 2 tablespoons lime juice
- 2 garlic cloves
- 2 tablespoons rice vinegar
- 2 tablespoons tamari

Method:

1. Whisk together all the soy, wine, lemon zest, garlic, corn syrup, and jalapenos in a small bowl.
2. Bring a small saucepan of salted water on the stove, and have an ice bath handy.
3. Put the rice, minced garlic, carrot, cucumbers, mangoes, bean sprouts, miso paste, and mint in the bowls.

5.8 Stir-Fried Noodles and Vegetables

Cooking Time: 20 minutes
Serving Size: 4

Ingredients:
Sauce

- 1 teaspoon sesame oil
- 1 teaspoon sugar
- 2 tablespoons light soy sauce
- 1 tablespoon dark soy sauce

Lo Mein

- 3 cups julienne-cut vegetables
- 2 tablespoons mirin
- 1 tablespoon sesame oil
- 3 green onions
- 6 ounces ramen noodles

Method:

1. In a jar, combine all of the sauce ingredients and shake well.
2. Cook the noodles as directed on the box.
3. Drain the water and put it aside.
4. In a large wok or pan, heat the sesame oil.
5. In a heated pan, add the spring onions and veggies.
6. Stir fry for five minutes, or until fork-tender.

7. To dislodge the browned pieces from the sides of the hole, add the mirin.
8. Toss in the fried rice and approximately half of the liquid in a heated pan to mix.
9. If necessary, add additional sauce.

5.9 Vegetarian Kimchi

Cooking Time: 1 day 16 hours

Serving Size: 15

Ingredients:

Chili Sauce

- 1 small white onion
- ½ cup red chili flake
- 1 head garlic
- 3 tablespoon fresh ginger

Vegan Fish Sauce

- 2 tablespoon coconut sugar
- 2 tablespoon tamari
- ¼ cup warm water
- ¼ cup pineapple juice

Cabbage

- 1 tablespoon Sea salt
- 1 head savoy cabbage

Vegetables

- 6 green onions
- 2 whole carrots

Method:

1. Begin by chopping up your dry and well-rinsed cauliflower.

2. Then, put your cabbage in a big mixing bowl and start packing a good quantity of sea salt between all leaves.

3. While your cabbage is resting, make your vegan salmon sauce by mixing all of the components in a small mixing dish.

4. Then, combine fresh ginger, garlic, onion, and red chili flake to make your chili sauce in a food processor or blender.

5. Toss in the vegan fish sauce and pulse to blend.

6. Meanwhile, combine the sliced carrots and spring onions (optional) with the sauce in a medium mixing dish.

7. Put the dried lettuce in the mixing bowl once it has been rinsed and dried.

8. Begin putting the coated lettuce leaves in the jar with clean hands.

5.10 Korean-Style Mapo Tofu

Cooking Time: 15 minutes

Serving Size: 2

Ingredients:

- ¼ green bell pepper
- ¼ red bell pepper
- 2 scallions
- 1 tablespoon garlic
- 4 ounces ground pork
- ½ medium onion
- 1 package tofu

Seasoning

- 2 teaspoons sesame oil
- 1 tablespoon starch
- ½ tablespoon gochujang
- 1 teaspoon sugar
- 2 tablespoons cooking oil
- 2 tablespoons soy sauce
- 1 tablespoon doenjang
- 1 tablespoon gochugaru

Method:

1. Prepare the veggies according to the instructions.
2. Two tablespoons of oil, heated in a large pan over medium-low heat.

3. Stir in the shallot, ½ of the sliced onion, garlic, and gochugaru for two or three minutes, or until aromatic.
4. Cook, mixing up the meat with a spoon until it is no lightly browned, two to three minutes.
5. Stir in the miso, gochujang, doenjang, and honey until the meat is well coated.
6. Cook for a few minutes until the bell peppers are somewhat softened.
7. To smooth the sauce, gently whisk in the starch slurry, followed by the sesame oil.
8. To bring everything together, cook for another minute or two.

5.11 Crispy Seaweed Noodle Rolls

Cooking Time: 30 minutes

Serving Size: 16

Ingredients:

- 10 stalks garlic chives
- cooking oil
- 1 fistful Korean glass noodles
- 1/3 carrot
- 8 dried seaweed sheets

Batter

- ¼ teaspoon fine sea salt
- ¾ cup water
- ½ cup potato starch
- ½ cup all-purpose flour

Sauce

- ¼ teaspoon sesame oil
- A few sprinkles of black pepper
- 1 teaspoon fine sea salt
- 1 tablespoon soy sauce

Method:

1. In a mixing dish, combine the noodles, vegetables, and garlic shallots.
2. Add the gravy and well combine it with your hands.

3. On seaweed sheets, place a tiny quantity of the glass noodle and veggie combination.
4. Roll the kelp into a ball.
5. To coat the rolled seaweed, place it in the batter dish.
6. In a wok, pour some oil.
7. Cook the seaweed wraps a second time for added crispiness.

5.12 Extra-Strong Fermented Soybean Paste

Cooking Time: 20 minutes

Serving Size: 4

Ingredients:

- 1 teaspoon Korean chili paste
- 1 teaspoon minced garlic
- 4½ cup dried kelp
- 3 tablespoon Korean soybean paste
- ½ small brown onion
- 250g Korean tofu
- 4 small shiitake mushrooms
- 1 pack enoki mushrooms
- ½ large zucchini

Method:

1. Begin by bringing the powdered kelp and dried anchovy stocks to a boil.
2. Turn down the heat to moderate and introduce the zucchini and onion after the stock has started to boil.
3. Boil for two or three minutes.
4. Boil for another 2 minutes after adding the tofu.
5. Boil for another 2 minutes after adding the shiitake and enoki mushrooms.

5.13 Knife-Cut Noodle Soup with Red Beans

Cooking Time: 2 hours

Serving Size: 4

Ingredients:

For the Soup

- ¼ medium onion
- 1 tablespoon soup soy sauce
- 2 white parts of scallions
- 1 3- inch dried kelp
- 1 small whole chicken
- 8 plump garlic cloves
- 4 ginger pieces
- ½ onion

For the Vegetables

- 1 medium zucchini
- 2 scallions

For the Chicken Meat

- 1 teaspoon sesame oil
- Salt and pepper
- 1 teaspoon minced garlic

For the Noodles

- 1 package noodles

Method:
1. Place the cleaned meat and ½ glasses of water in a stockpot big enough to accommodate both the chicken and the water.
2. Combine the onion, cloves, ginger, shallots, and ½ cups water in a large mixing bowl.
3. Over moderate heat, stir it to a boil.
4. Season the sauteed zucchini for approximately 15 minutes before squeezing out the excess water.
5. Remove the extra fat from the broth by straining it.
6. Bring the soup back to a boil in the pot.
7. Add the dried kelp, onion pieces, and soup soy sauce, if desired.
8. Bring to a boil, then reduce to low heat for a few minutes.
9. Season to taste with salt and pepper.
10. Meanwhile, heat water in a separate pot to parboil the pasta.
11. Stir in the noodle mixture.
12. To serve, pour the noodle and broth into a serving dish, then top with the chicken, zucchini, and scallion slices.

5.14 Steamed Perilla Leaves

Cooking Time: 10 minutes

Serving Size: 10

Ingredients:
Sauce

- 1 tablespoon perilla oil
- 2 teaspoon sesame seeds
- ½ cup onion
- 1 tablespoon red chili powder
- 3 tablespoon cooking's sake
- ½ cup green onions
- ¾ cup water
- 4 teaspoon anchovy sauce
- Two tablespoons apple-lemon soy sauce

Method:

1. Perilla leaves should be washed and drained.
2. They should be layered so that they can dry quickly.
3. Make the seasoning sauce by combining all of the sauce components in a dish; stack three leaves in the pan.
4. Top the Perilla leaf with 1-2 spoonfuls of the sauce.
5. Add another stack of three perilla leaves to the pan, but this time flip it 180 degrees.
6. Cover the saucepan and simmer the leaves for approximately two minutes or 1 ½ minute on moderate flame.

7. Serve it as a dipping sauce with grains and other meals, warm, room temperature, or even cold.

5.15 Omija Punch with Pear

Cooking Time: 12 hours

Serving Size: 6

Ingredients:
- Honey or sugar
- Korean pear
- 1-liter water
- 10g dried schisandra berry

Method:
1. In a small bowl, soak the dried omija in ice water up overnight.
2. Remove the berries from the filter and toss them out (keeping the liquid).
3. If desired, sweeten with honey or sugar.
4. You may also add additional Korean pear chunks if desired. Serve.

5.16 Beet Jelly Candy

Cooking Time: 1 hour

Serving Size: 8

Ingredients:

Pickled Beet Jelly

- 5 teaspoon of gelatin
- ½ cup of cold water
- 2/3 cup of Pickled Beet Juice
- 8.8 oz Pickled Juice

Method:

1. Process the tonic water and beetroot together until smooth.
2. Strain the liquid through a fine filter to remove the debris.
3. Meanwhile, in a dish, pour the cold water and scatter the jelly over it.
4. Allow about fifteen minutes for the gelatin to bloom.
5. In a saucepan, pour the beet water and heat that until it begins to boil.
6. Remove from the fire and whisk for a few moments before adding the gelatin that has bloomed.
7. Lightly coat a quarter pan with nonstick oil or line it with a Silpat.
8. Wrap the tray with bubble wrap after pouring the beet juice on it.

5.17 Vegetable and Fruit Water Kimchi

Cooking Time: 30 minutes
Serving Size: 4

Ingredients:

- Salt
- 1-gallon airtight container
- 8 stalks of minari
- 5 plump garlic cloves
- 1.5-pound Korean radish
- ½ Korean pear
- 3 thin scallions
- 1.5 tablespoons gochugaru
- 1 medium carrot
- 12 napa cabbage

Method:

1. Scrub the radishes with a brush to wash them.
2. Cut the discs into 1-inch-thick discs.
3. Several times wash the cabbage stems.
4. Combine with the radish in a mixing basin.
5. Toss in two tablespoons of salt and toss well to spread the salt evenly.
6. Steep the gochugaru in 2 cups of warm water in the bottom dish.
7. Other veggies should be cut into 1-inch lengths.
8. Combine with the seasoned radish and lettuce in a mixing bowl.

9. Dissolve two teaspoons salt in ten cups water in a large mixing basin.
10. Using a fine-mesh strainer, strain the drenched gochugaru into the liquid.
11. Spill the marinade over the marinated radish and cabbage mixture and stir everything together well.
12. Maintain it in an enclosed room or container.

5.18 Spicy Stuffed Steamed Eggplant

Cooking Time: 15 minutes

Serving Size: 4

Ingredients:
- 4 long, purple eggplants

For Stuffing
- 2 teaspoon neutral oil
- 1 tablespoon Asian sesame oil
- ½ teaspoon sugar
- 1 tablespoon sesame
- 1 teaspoon minced garlic
- ½ teaspoon gochugaru
- ½ cup spring onion
- ½ cup onion
- 3 tablespoon gochujang

Method:
1. Heat 2 teaspoons of any neutral oil, such as rice straw, in a skillet.

2. Add one teaspoon sauteed garlic and ½ teaspoon thinly sliced onions.
3. Add spice ingredients.
4. Fill a steamer or pressure cooker halfway with water.
5. Set the heat to high and allow the water to begin to simmer.
6. Stuff each eggplant with a large quantity of the Gochujang-flavored filling.
7. In a big vessel, place the filled eggplants.
8. 15 minutes of steaming eggplants
9. Remove the Gochujang Gaji-jjim from the steamer and set it aside.
10. Some of the fillings may have settled to the bottom of the container.

5.19 Spicy, Chewy, Sweet & Sour Cold Noodles

Cooking Time: 25 minutes

Serving Size: 4

Ingredients:

- Onion
- 1 tablespoon toasted sesame seeds
- 1 tablespoon white sugar
- 1 tablespoon white vinegar
- 3 bundles style noodles
- ½ teaspoon fish sauce
- 2 tablespoon hot pepper paste

- ½ large-sized carrot
- 1 cup Kimchi
- 2 pickling cucumbers

Method:
1. Using a sharp knife, shave the kimchi into extremely thin slices.
2. Cook the pasta according to package directions.
3. Let's make the spicy gochujang sauce while the pasta is cooking.
4. In a medium bowl, combine the sugars, gochujang, shrimp paste, and wine and put them away later.
5. Drain the noodles into a strainer, rinse thoroughly, and drain well.
6. Serve and have fun!

5.20 Braised Lotus Roots

Cooking Time: 30 minutes

Serving Size: 8

Ingredients:
- 1 tablespoon vinegar
- ½ teaspoon sesame seeds
- 1 pound lotus roots

For the Braising Liquid
- 2 tablespoons corn syrup
- ½ tablespoon sesame oil
- 2 tablespoons sugar
- 1 tablespoon cooking oil

- 2 tablespoons rice wine
- 4 tablespoons soy sauce

Method:
1. Cut the rough ends off the lotus root and use a potato peeler to scrape the skin off.
2. In a medium-sized saucepan, combine the lotus root slices with just enough salted water and a teaspoon of wine.
3. Bring to a boil, then reduce to low heat and simmer for ten minutes, undisturbed.
4. Put them back in the pot.
5. Combine 1 cup water, sesame oil, white wine, honey, and canola oil in a mixing bowl.
6. Bring the water to a boil.
7. Three to five minutes after adding the cane sugar and soy sauce, stir well.
8. Keep any leftovers in the refrigerator.
9. When serving, coat the bottom of the dish with the sauce.

Conclusion

Beef and other meat, by comparison, is used carefully, which magnifies the health benefits of Korean cuisine. The Koreans choose lean and balanced forms, such as lean ground beef, chicken thighs, and oily fish, even though it is a full meal. Consequently, due to lower dietary fat and cholesterol levels in Korean cuisine, the chances for heart disease are substantially lower. The safe styles are the preparation equipment, methods, and tools used for making Korean food. The most common ways to prepare Korean cuisine are roasting, stir-frying, simmering and fermenting, implying that the foods are prepared in their fluids.

In comparison, in the country with greater obesity rates, such as the United States, many products are deep-fried in oil containers. In transition, typically, food and medicine are viewed as one, and the same thing is considered in Korea. Their belief that wellbeing begins with food suggests that if any result is not shown after attempting to cure all ailments first with food, medical care should be attempted. The Korean people's meals are associated with being good and delightful. They have developed from the history, nature of the region, and customs of the people of the Korean peninsula through varying features over the years. The Koreans have produced fermentation foods that promote metabolism to keep the body hot and safe. The scientific background of the local Korean cuisine growing for centuries is based on this knowledge. Thus Korean meals have all benefits in their ingredients and spices. Try these quick and straightforward recipes discussed in the book and make your meals as tasty as you want using Korean food preparation techniques.